I0086871

A Side of Sunlight

Is There Sunlight on Your Plate?

This book belongs to

_____

My thanks to the following:

My angel, for being my inspiration.

My lion, for being my joy.

My heart, for being my partner.

My biggest fan, for being my cheerleader.

My favorite person, for being my counselor.

My "BIG" brother, for being my guide.

And to those who lent a willing ear and cheered me on.

Copyright © 2015 Lillian Aharon Designs, Inc.
All rights reserved.
ISBN: 0-6925-11180
ISBN-13: 978-0-692-51118-3

Included in the appendix:

- Questions for discussion -

- A note from the author -

- Information about the different -
phytonutrients found in food

- Organic vs. non-organic -

- USDA recommendations for a healthy plate -

"Yes, I like the color green,"
said Oliver so proudly.

"But on leaves and shirts and cars,"
which he added much too loudly.

Well, he sat there kind of smug,
which his mother thought was funny,

As his sister, Eve, waved the broccoli,
singing *yummy yummy yummy*.

"You should try to eat more sunlight,"
his mother said waving her hand.

What the sun had to do with food,
Oliver didn't understand.

"Will you try it again?" his mother asked.
"Your little sister loves to eat it.

"Hey, where's that veggie book Dad bought?
We really ought to read it.

"Let's look at the book and then you'll see,
why sunlight is so ideal.

"It can make you healthy and strong,
when you eat it with every meal."

Oliver went to get the book,
but came back in with a frown.

"Why so glum?" asked his mother,
as he set the new book down.

"I like to read about things," he said.
"You know, like stuff that makes me think."

Oliver sat down with a huff,
and his mother gave him a wink.

"Don't you like science and nature?" she asked.
"I know that you like the weather.

"Do you know what can happen
when we put those things together?"

And then a smile touched his face,
and his thinking had begun.

"We get plants and food," she answered.
"But more importantly, the sun."

His mother pointed to the broccoli,
"This veggie's green and sugar-free,

"But if you look at it more closely,
you'll see it looks just like a tree!

"It grows from soil on the ground,
and gets energy from the sun.

"Okay, let's look at this book,
I think it could be fun!

"We're all powered by sunlight," she read.
"Energy is what it's about.

"But people can't eat the sun's rays,
so we need something to help us out.

Learn more about *photosynthesis*, *phytonutrients* and *solar panels* at the end of the book

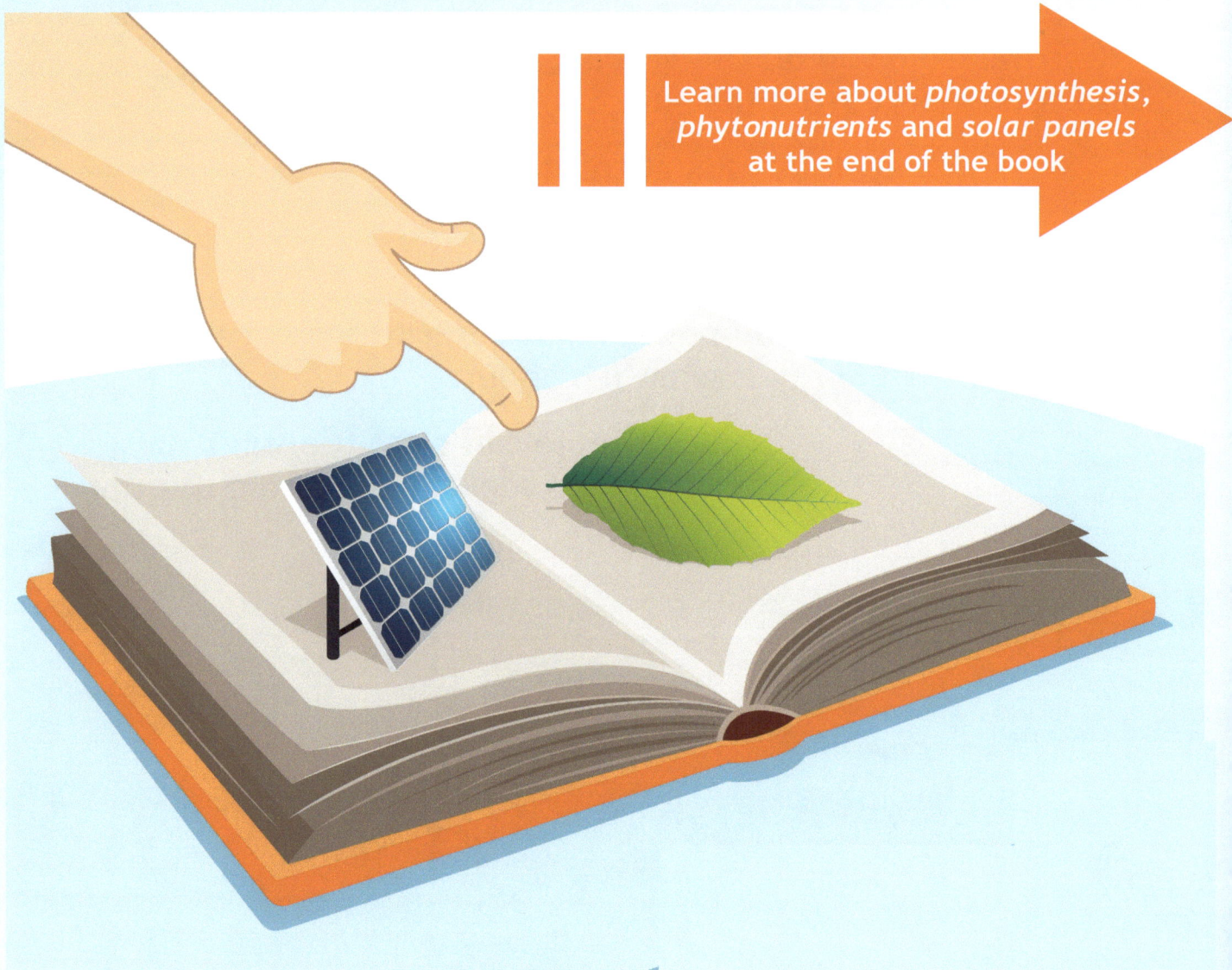

"It says here 'photosynthesis',
now that's a really big word.

"And also 'phytonutrients',
I think that's one you've never heard.

"Now take a look at a leaf,
it looks like a solar panel.

"The book says it absorbs the sun
and produces something we can handle.

"Sunlight helps the plants grow
and then they hold the light for you.

"And when you eat a fruit or vegetable,
your body uses the sun like fuel."

Oliver closed the book Dad got,
and his mother knew he understood,

That eating sunlight everyday,
can make us feel really good!

With some broccoli on the table
and some apples in a bowl,

Oliver wanted to eat better,
it was his new worthwhile goal.

His mother was delighted
when he finally took a bite.

It was worth another try,
he knew his mother had been right.

He closed his eyes and imagined
vegetables growing in the ground,

And with every bite he took
he felt his thoughts turning round.

There was sunshine in his mouth
and while he imagined this was true,

He thought about the fuel in food
and all the things that it could do.

"There's so much food to choose from," she said.
"Just some are healthier than others.

"It's good to eat all types of things,
in different shapes, sizes and colors.

———

"Just be sure that fruits or veggies
are a part of every meal.

"Your choices are important
when they affect how well you feel.

"So if you eat something tasty,
but it can sit up on a shelf,

"You'll ask yourself, '*Can this fuel me?*'
and '*Is this good for my health?*'"

———————

"I really get it!" Oliver laughed.
and his mother said, "That's great!"

*"Now everyday I'll ask myself,
'Is there sunlight on my plate?'"*

1. Can you name some foods that have sunlight in them?

2. What is your favorite fruit? What is your favorite vegetable?

3. What does eating the sunlight found in food do for your health?

4. How many fruits and vegetables do you think you should have on your plate at mealtime?

5. Besides fruits or vegetables, what are some other types of foods that are healthy for us?

6. Would you like to try a different color fruit or vegetable, like a green kiwi or a purple potato?

7. What would you put in a fruit or vegetable smoothie? What vegetables would you put in your favorite bowl of soup?

8. If you could go to the supermarket and pick out your own fruits and vegetables, which would you choose? *Challenge*: Pick out as many as there are colors in the rainbow.

9. How would you design a colorful fruit and vegetable platter that you can serve to your friends or family? Challenge: Use as many colors and shapes as you can to create a work of art. Check out asideofsunlight.com to find creative ways for kids to make food art. Learn how to design flowers, smiley faces, animals and so much more!

10. If you could describe your personality or looks as a fruit or vegetable, which would you be? Why?

Comments

- When children get into the kitchen and see how their food is prepared, or even prepare some of the food themselves, they may be more likely to eat it.

- Oftentimes, when given an opportunity to create a vegetable platter for their parents, siblings or friends, children will take so much pride in their effort that they may eat some of the vegetables themselves.

- Serving familiar foods next to ones they've never tried is a good way to introduce something new. On the other hand, you may also want to try serving something new *before* serving something you know they will like. In this way, they may consider eating the new food because they are hungry and it won't be competing with any other food on their plate.

I hope you enjoy reading this book as much as I enjoyed writing it. The truth is, this book was created out of frustration. I had a very hard time clearly explaining to my children the concept of eating healthfully, in a way that their young minds would understand. One of my sons would present various bags of snacks and tell me that because it showed a picture of a vegetable on it, it must be healthy. This made me realize that I didn't have the language necessary to convey the importance of food in its natural form, fresh and unprocessed.

Thus was born the concept of "sunlight in food." We now have a routine in my family: One of my children will ask for something specific to eat and then I will respond by asking, "How much sunlight is in that?" If the answer is "none" or "not much," they know it's not the best choice. While I know there are many types of healthy foods available, like nuts, beans, herbs, fish, eggs and poultry to name a few, I would really like for fruits and vegetables to be the foundation of their diet.

The language presented in this book has changed our lives. In the past, my kids thought I was randomly assigning good or bad labels to food. Now they understand my thought process. I can safely say they no longer believe that I'm punishing them when I ask them to make a better choice.

Every once in a while, my son will indulge me and tell me that he can feel the sunlight in his mouth and he imagines the food has become a group of soldiers running through his body, fighting viruses and infection. It puts a smile on my face to know that he understands what healthy food does for him.

As a nation, we can no longer sit back and watch our children be confused by food labels while they, and we, try to understand lists of unpronounceable ingredients. We know that if a food can sit up on a shelf for a lengthy period of time or if it has been through a processing plant, then it may not be the best choice for our bodies and minds.

It is my hope that this book will help everyone — children and adults alike. We should all be asking ourselves: **Is there sunlight in this food?** Is this food in its most natural state? Asking these questions will allow us to redirect our healthy compass and bring healthy eating back into our families and our nation as a whole.

With much love and care,

Jillian

Feel free to visit: ASideOfSunlight.com

The Phytonutrients in Food

Did you know that fruits and vegetables have to work very hard to survive when exposed to harsh elements, such as extreme hot or cold temperatures, wind, rain, insects or harmful UV radiation?

Phytonutrients help to protect the plant. The more that a plant has to fight, the tougher its immune system becomes. The chemical reaction that takes place within the plant, as well as it's struggle to survive, is what makes fruits and vegetables so good for us. It's fascinating to learn that the immunity a plant develops is transferred to us when we eat it, allowing us to fight off toxins in our body as well. This means that when we eat a fruit or a vegetable, we are consuming a fighting machine whose enemies are inflammation, aging, viruses and bacteria. Some of the best fruits and vegetables are the brightest ones because the more color they have, the more phytonutrients they contain. Here is a list of some of the different color categories and the phytonutrients and health benefits affiliated with them:

WHITE OR BROWN FOOD

Onions, pears, cauliflower, garlic, ginger • *Because these foods don't have much color, you may think that they are not powerful, but they are very nutrient rich!* Some phytonutrients: Allicin, indoles, glucosinolates. Some health benefits: Supports healthy bones, circulatory system and arterial function. Fights heart disease and cancer.*

BLUE OR PURPLE FOOD

Purple grapes, plums, eggplant, acai berry, blackberry, wild blueberry, elderberry. Some phytonutrients: Resveratrol, anthocyanidins, and phenolics. Some health benefits: Good for heart, brain, bone, arteries and cognitive health. Fights cancer and supports healthy aging.*

RED OR PINK FOOD

Raspberry, strawberry, cherry, cranberry, pomegranate, red cabbage, red bell pepper, radishes, tomato, watermelon, guava, pink grapefruit, cayenne pepper. Some phytonutrients: Lycopene, ellagic acid, anthocyanidins. Some health benefits: Supports prostate, urinary tract and DNA health. Protects against cancer and heart disease.*

ORANGE OR YELLOW FOOD

Cantaloupe, apricots, papaya, peaches, mango, yellow & orange bell peppers, carrots, sweet potatoes, squash, turmeric. Some phytonutrients: Alpha-carotene, beta-carotene, beta cryptoxanthin, lutein. Some health benefits: Good for eye health, healthy immune function, healthy growth and development.*

DARK GREEN FOOD

Leafy greens and cruciferous vegetables like kale, parsley, spinach, collard greens, brussels sprouts, broccoli, green tea, oregano. Some phytonutrients: Lutein, indoles, isothiocyanates, sulforaphane. Some health benefits: Supports eye health, arterial function, lung health, liver function and cell health.*

* Please refer to disclaimer

Organic Vs. Non-Organic

Is organic better than non-organic for your family?

This question can be very difficult to answer. My best advice would be to conduct your own research and formulate your own opinion. Ask friends and family who are close to you. If there are public figures that you trust, maybe look up their philosophies on the subject. I know that a common argument against buying organic food is the extra cost, although organic produce and products are more readily available today than ever before and overall prices have become more affordable. You should know that it doesn't have to be an "all or nothing" decision. You could very well decide that some organic products might be worth the investment over others depending on pesticide exposure levels and how much of it your family eats. Keep in mind, however, that buying organic is not just about pesticides; it's about supporting farming practices that are environmentally friendly, minimizing soil erosion, safeguarding workers and protecting wildlife, water quality and more. So, do some research and ask around. You'll eventually make a decision and whatever decision you make will be the right one for your family.

The USDA (United States Department of Agriculture) has developed a certification that helps to identify foods that are organic. Companies and farmers need to adhere to certain guidelines to receive this certification, such as:

Some USDA Organic Guidelines

Produce	They may not use synthetic chemicals such as pesticides (although some organic produce may use biological pesticides that have been approved by the government)
Livestock	Special guidelines for feeding, housing and breeding must be followed

Organic According to the USDA

100% Organic	Product must be completely organic
Organic	Product must be at least 95% organic
Made with Organic Ingredients	Product must be at least 70% organic

To learn more, go to www.usda.gov

PHOTOSYNTHESIS

Photosynthesis means
"putting together with light."

It's the process that allows some plants to
survive by turning sunlight energy into food energy.

PHYTONUTRIENTS

"Phyto" is from the Greek word *phyton* meaning "plant".

Scientists discovered that the phytonutrients in plants
help them resist disease and drought.

When we eat those fruits and vegetables,
our bodies are also able to help fight disease.

SOLAR PANELS

Solar panels are made of silicon. When sunlight
shines on the panel, it holds the sunlight
(just like a leaf holds sunlight).

The silicon then creates energy that can be used.

For more on:

√ **How to build a healthy plate at meal time**

√ **Nutritional tips**

√ **Eating better on a budget**

√ **Understanding Nutrition Facts Labels**

√ **And much more, visit:**

www.ChooseMyPlate.gov

This website was created by the U.S. Department of Agriculture. Their first action-prompting message is:

"MAKE HALF YOUR PLATE FRUITS AND VEGETABLES"

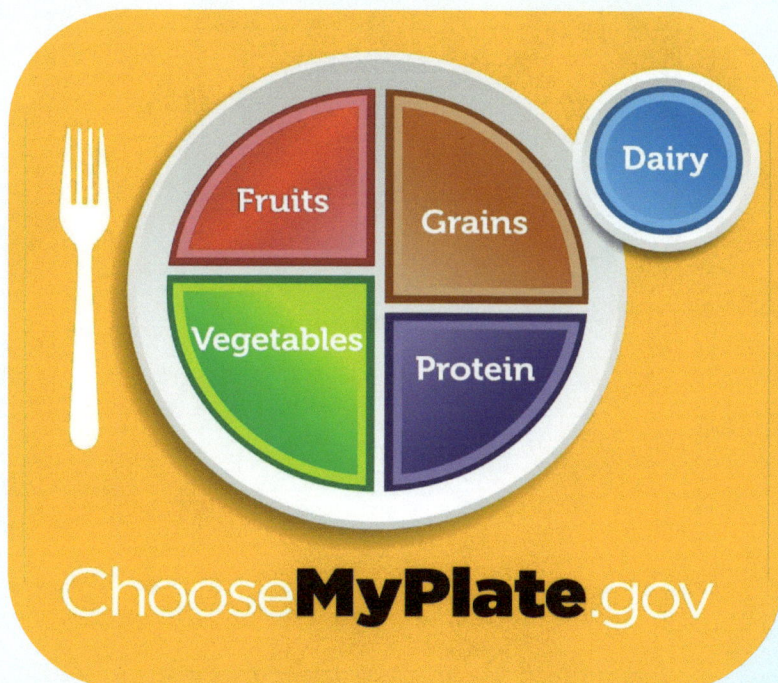

Oliver

&

Eve

A Side of Sunlight

Is There Sunlight on Your Plate?

*Disclaimer:

This book is presented solely for educational and entertainment purposes. Its contents have not been vetted by the U.S. Food and Drug Administration, or any other health-related, regulatory agency. This book should not be used as a substitute for the recommendations of a qualified health care professional. Neither the author nor the publisher shall be held liable or responsible to any person or entity relative to any loss or damage sustained, or alleged to have been sustained, directly or indirectly, as a result of this publication or its contents. Always consult with a licensed, qualified health care professional before altering or participating in any dietary program.

About the Author

Born in Los Angeles and raised in Chicago, Lillian Strauss Aharon spent most of her childhood with her nose in a book. She began reading and writing poetry at a young age. This, together with a passion for singing and song writing, led her to receive a degree in English Literature.

Lillian's parents have always been motivating, supportive and creative. Along with the best brother a sister could ever hope for, they encouraged her to follow her dreams, whether they were to become a singer, artist, wife, mother, teacher or writer.

Lillian now lives in Boca Raton, Florida and is happily married to her best friend, Joey. They have two amazing boys, who ask way too many questions, but inevitably force her to come up with answers. She has always had an intense desire to help children and adults reach their potential in a joyful and peaceful way.

www.ingramcontent.com/pod-product-compliance
Lightning Source LLC
Chambersburg PA
CBHW041242040426
42445CB00004B/124